beginner's guide to buddhist
meditation

beginner's guide to buddhist
meditation
practices for mindful living

CHRISTINA FELDMAN

Rodmell Press
Berkeley, California
2006

Beginner's Guide to Buddhist Meditation: Practices for Mindful Living,
copyright © 2006 by Axis Publishing.

Conceived and created by
Axis Publishing
8c Accommodation Road
London NW11 8ED
www.axispublishing.co.uk

This edition published by
Rodmell Press
2147 Blake Street
Berkeley, CA 94704
www.rodmellpress.com

Creative Director: Siân Keogh
Editorial Director: Anne Yelland
Designer: Simon de Lotz
Production: Jo Ryan, Cécile Lerbière

Library of Congress Cataloging-in-
Publication Data

Feldman, Christina.
  Beginner's guide to Buddhist meditation :
practices for mindful living / Christina
Feldman.
    p. cm.
  Includes index.
  ISBN-13: 978-1-930485-13-6 (first
edition : alk. paper)
  1. Meditation--Buddhism. I. Title.
  BQ5602.F45 2006
  294.3'4435—dc22
                        2006015159

Printed in China

First Edition

ISBN 10: 1-930485-13-1
ISBN 13: 978-1-930485-13-6

10 09 08 07 06 1 2 3 4 5

Distributed by Publishers Group West

contents

beginner's guide to buddhist meditation

introduction

Meditation is a powerful way of discovering the calm, sensitivity, happiness, and compassion we yearn for in our lives. The serenity, insight, and openheartedness we long for are born of a clear mind and receptive heart. The Buddha's teaching of meditation is simple and profound, rooted in the moment-to-moment realities of our lives.

The path of meditation teaches us to turn toward our lives, bodies, minds, and hearts. Wherever we are in our lives, whoever we are in this moment is where the path of wisdom and compassion begins. In the midst of events and changes in our life, we learn the

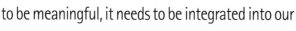

power of wise attention, kindness, and the ways to find balance and simplicity. The inner freedom, respect, and integrity that transform our lives grow from our willingness to meet our life wholeheartedly.

This book is intended to help you begin on a meditative path. The range of meditation practices within it offer ways of learning to live a more easeful, peaceful, and connected life. A meditative life is cultivated not only in seclusion; for it to be meaningful, it needs to be integrated into our

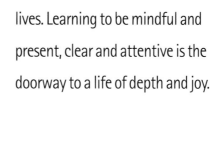

lives. Learning to be mindful and present, clear and attentive is the doorway to a life of depth and joy.

1

first thoughts

The Buddha taught that meditation is "a path of happiness that leads to the highest happiness." There is no end to the meditative process: it is a lifelong practice that can be undertaken by anyone, regardless of age and spiritual beliefs, and there is no right or wrong time to start on your meditative path. This chapter explores the basics of meditation, and what you might learn as you take the first steps on your path to happiness.

what is meditation?

Meditation is a timeless path that lies at the heart of all great spiritual traditions. Throughout time, people have sought places and times of seclusion in monasteries, temples, deserts, and on mountaintops, trying to find a way to discover inner stillness, a sense of the sacred, and spiritual renewal. The art of meditation is deeply rooted in ancient spiritual paths, yet it is equally relevant and transforming for people today. In contemporary meditation centers, in people's homes, and in the midst of busy and committed lives, countless people cultivate a contemplative path.

The various ways of practicing meditation are no longer seen as esoteric exercises for a select elite, but are increasingly being integrated into every aspect of our culture, and are becoming a central part of many people's lives. Countless people, dedicating themselves to a life of deep wisdom and compassion, reserve time and space in their days to cultivate the same stillness, peace, and understanding as the great masters and meditators of the past used to do.

The central message of meditation is not bound by religion, culture, or time. When we live in a world that seems to offer escalating levels of demand, busyness, and expectation, paths that teach us ways of discovering greater inner peace, calmness, insight, and transformation become increasingly valuable and relevant. We come to understand that it is not always possible or even desirable to disengage from lives of creativity, commitment, and relatedness, but it is always possible for us to transform our hearts and minds. Our deep-rooted longings for peace, intimacy, compassion, sensitivity, and understanding are timeless and enduring.

learning from meditation

Meditation is not concerned with the performance of rituals, having transcendent experiences, or even attaining altered states of consciousness. These may be a dimension of some meditative disciplines, yet the central teaching of meditation is much simpler.

■ Are we living our lives with the generosity, kindness, and sensitivity that they ask of us?

■ Are we able to meet both adversity and alienation with compassion and understanding?

■ Are we able to be at ease with the events of our own minds and bodies?

■ Can we cultivate peace amid the chaos that can touch our lives?

These are the questions that lie at the heart of the Buddha's teaching.

We learn through meditation and mindfulness to place our deepest longings and aspirations for peace, stillness, and transformation at the center of our lives. We discover what it means to be increasingly awake and present in the midst of the joys and difficulties that life brings to us. The qualities of compassion and sensitivity become increasingly accessible and can deeply transform all the moments we feel isolated, lost, and disengaged. We learn how to let go of obsession and confusion, and balance the emotional and psychological storms that can disable us.

The classroom of meditation is life itself—our relationships, work, families, and commitments. The lessons of peace, calmness, and understanding are learned in our bodies, minds, and hearts.

EXPERIENCE

Meditation practice is not theoretical but experiential. The deepening and effectiveness of our meditation relies on our own willingness to cultivate and develop it as a practice and path in every moment and circumstance life brings.

AWARENESS

Through learning to be increasingly attentive and present, we become deeply aware of the life of our mind, heart, and body. We awaken to the ways that we affect our world on a moment-to-moment level and the ways we are affected by the world around us. This sensitivity and wakefulness is the starting point of a meditative path.

UNDERSTANDING

Central to the Buddhist path is the understanding that we cannot avoid aging, sickness, or death. We cannot avoid all loss, sorrow, and heartache, and the endeavor to do so only magnifies pain. We do begin to see that confusion, agitation, fear, and stress may become optional in our lives.

TRANSFORMATION

We begin to understand that our lives do not need to be governed by impulsive and habitual reactions. All transformation and our capacity to travel new pathways of peace and understanding in our lives begin with awareness.

meditation in everyday life

Meditation is not entirely new to any of us. We have all had glimpses of deep calm and stillness in our lives. Moments of startling insight, profound and heightened sensitivity are not strangers to any of us. We have experienced the capacity of our minds to be overwhelmingly distressed and the capacity of our minds to be collected, clear, and calm. We have seen that our capacity for rage, fear, and mistrust lives side by side with our capacity for love, compassion, and generosity. Meditation teaches us that these glimpses and moments of serenity, stillness, and depth do not need to be random accidents in our lives. We learn to cultivate and nurture the potential we have for greatness of heart and stillness of mind. The encouragement and willingness to be more present and awake in our lives enable us to embrace the reality of the present and approach the future with greater kindness, balance, and clarity.

THE MEANING OF MEDITATION

1 Meditation is both simple and profound, both mystical and practical.

2 The path of awakening begins with our willingness to approach who and where we are in our life with greater attention and sensitivity.

3 We learn to leave no moment in our life unattended and discover the ways in which awareness illuminates our life both inwardly and outwardly.

4 We discover that peace, a sense of sacredness and stillness do not lie on some distant horizon, but in the moment and life we are living.

5 We discover what it means to be a conscious participant in healing our bodies, opening our hearts, and stilling our minds.

6 The changes and transformations we encounter within ourselves inevitably affect the nature of our relationships, our creativity, and the quality of life we experience.

7 The benefits of deepening awareness in our life are not solely personal. Our world calls out for greater compassion, peace, and understanding.

This book is a guide to meditation, offering the essential guidelines that will enable anyone to begin to cultivate greater awareness and presence in their life. Meditative teaching is not an exhortation or demand but an invitation to explore the ways of walking new paths of mindfulness and wakefulness. It is an invitation to discover a deeper well-being and inner richness that can transform every aspect of our lives. We already have everything we need to take the first steps on this path—a body, mind, heart, and the willingness to explore what it means to live with greater depth, wholeheartedness, and sensitivity.

2

meditation basics

There is no right or wrong time or place to meditate. Establishing a quiet corner for meditation and the practice of meditating at a similar time each day can be helpful for many beginners on the path. The questions of when, where, and how often will be answered through experience and experimentation. The answers will be different for every person traveling on the path. Meditation deepens through practice and dedication.

how to meditate

The Buddha encouraged the cultivation of mindfulness whether a student is sitting, standing, walking, or lying down. He suggested that his students set aside periods of solitude and silence for contemplation, reflection, and formal meditation. Equally, he encouraged them to approach their work, relationships, speech, and interaction with the world as opportunities to deepen in wisdom and compassion.

cultivating sensitivity

Meditation is not just something we "do." It is the cultivation of sensitivity, balance, attentiveness, and understanding in every area of our life. On its deepest level, meditation is a way of seeing and being. We learn to cultivate mindfulness in the moments we are most disconnected, sensitivity in the places that are most habitual, and calm in the midst of chaos.

No one person's meditation practice is consistently profound, filled with startling insight and wondrous experiences, simply because no one's mind is like this. There will be times when our meditation practice is calm and rich, and also times when it will feel flat or difficult. The essence of a meditation path is the unconditional willingness to be present with the whole spectrum of our life experience, both inwardly and outwardly. We learn to attend equally to the pleasant and the unpleasant, the delightful and the challenging. Perseverance and dedication are great allies in the deepening of meditation. With practice, there begins to emerge a reliable clarity and calmness that nothing can shatter.

choosing a retreat

Countless people find it beneficial to participate in formal meditation retreats to deepen their practice. A sustained period of meditation, whether a day, a weekend, a week or longer, offers the opportunity to explore in depth our capacities for awareness and understanding.

Being in a community of practitioners in a contemplative environment allows us to disentangle from the world, to let go of busyness, and find within ourselves a refuge of stillness. It is equally helpful and transforming to integrate dedicated periods of stillness and meditation into our lives. Our lives and commitments do not always easily lend themselves to taking extended periods of time away.

We learn to bring our meditation practice into our lives, creating sanctuaries of calm in the midst of all the demands of our lives. We learn that we cannot afford to neglect the quality of our heart and mind. The stillness, clarity, compassion, and equanimity we nurture within ourselves impact upon and transform every area of our life.

when to meditate

It is not possible to prescribe the "correct" amount of time that any one of us should dedicate to practicing meditation. What we can do is create a specific time in our day which we commit to the cultivation of our practice. Many people find it useful to begin their day with a time of calm collectedness. It is equally useful to end the day with a period of stillness. The thought that something else is more pressing arises often. We remember that there is no more important task in our life than caring for the quality of our hearts and minds: these are at the forefront of everything else in our life. As we begin to embed these periods of stillness into our life, increasingly we see and welcome the benefits they bring.

It is useful to commit a minimum period of time to your meditation session: it can be 20 minutes, 30 minutes, or longer. It is not only a commitment to time, but also to being as wholeheartedly present as you are able to be within the life of your body, mind, and present moment. It is a commitment to being where you are, with whatever the moment brings, instead of leaning forward into the future or replaying the events of the past. It is a commitment to mindfulness and befriending the moment rather than following pathways of resistance, distraction, or avoidance.

In the Buddhist tradition, there is the encouragement "when you sit, just sit, when you walk, just walk, when you eat, just eat. Above all don't wobble." Learning not to wobble is one of the first lessons we learn on the path.

getting a routine going

It may take some time to find the routine that suits you best, and it is important that you are not discouraged

SECRETS OF GOOD MEDITATION

1 If you have only a short time available for formal meditation, it can be useful to develop the simple practice of focusing on your breath as a means to establish yourself in the moment.

2 Each moment of returning your attention to your breath is a moment of letting go. When you breathe with mindfulness, you integrate your mind, body, and the present moment.

3 Each time you connect with just one breath at a time you are cultivating simplicity and calm. If you continue to practice, you will see that greater calmness, kindness, and clarity pervade your life.

by any initial difficulty you have with this. There may be times when you sit in meditation only to find yourself besieged by thoughts of what you need to attend to in your day or the things you have left undone. These are the moments we remember the patience and dedication required to cultivate a heart and mind of ease.

restlessness and ease

At times of great restlessness, you may be tempted to conclude that your meditation is worthless and unproductive. It is important to remember that all these small moments you endeavor to pay attention rather than being lost, to be awake rather than entangled in agitation are all worthy moments. You are remembering something too important to forget: how to live wholeheartedly and attend to what is right before you. There will be countless times you will be asked to begin again and renew your intention to be present. Each moment we are able to do this is a change of heart and mind that will, with practice, change your life. In your meditation, as in your life, you will have to choose over and over whether to follow the paths of impatience, judgment, frustration, and complexity, or the pathways of patience, acceptance, balance, and simplicity. Increasingly, you will come to understand that the choice lies in your own heart.

where to meditate

In the same way that we need to establish a regular time of day for formal meditation, it is also helpful to establish a place or setting that is as supportive as possible. Aim to create an environment that, as much as possible, is simple, uncluttered, and quiet, in which you are able to give care and attention to your inner landscape. Be willing to turn off your television and telephone. Aim to cultivate an environment of seclusion and simplicity.

a calm corner

A setting, even if it is just a corner of your bedroom that is dedicated to calm simplicity, is a visible reminder of our own longing to nurture inner simplicity and serenity. It is rarely possible to create a space that is entirely devoid of sound and objects, nor is it necessary to do so. It is possible to cultivate dedicated spaces of calm outwardly that remind us to cultivate an oasis of calm within our own hearts and minds.

MEDITATION POSTURES

Like all those beginning on their path, you will have seen images of Buddhas seated in a full lotus posture looking totally at ease, assuming that this is the ideal way to practice. There is no one posture that is a direct path to enlightenment. In much the same way that there is no one "correct" way to meditate, there is no one posture that must be adopted. What is most important is to find a posture you can sustain and be still within.

1 Meditation practice rarely deepens if it is turned into an ongoing struggle or battle with pain and discomfort. It is most helpful to find a posture in which you can relax and be at ease.

2 At the same time, if your posture is alert, poised, and upright, it is a visible reminder of the qualities of heart and mind you are endeavoring to cultivate. Let your back and neck be upright, and your hands, face, and shoulders soft and relaxed.

3 You can sit on a meditation cushion, bench, or chair. Experiment until you find a posture in which your body feels balanced and at ease. Let your hands rest on your legs or together. Your eyes can be closed or just softly gazing at the floor in front of you.

4 Spend a few moments at the beginning of each meditation checking in with your body, aware of the places your body contacts the ground, cushion, or chair, aware of the uprightness of your back and neck, and consciously softening any places in your body where you are carrying tension or tightness.

5 If illness or chronic pain prevent you from being upright in your posture, do not think this is an obstacle. Find a lying posture in which you can be still and relaxed. The alertness within your posture can be found by lying with your knees bent and your feet flat on the floor or by raising one of your forearms off the floor. Your eyes can be open or closed, whatever is most conducive to being awake and present.

interest

Wise attention will always follow wise intention and wise intention is born of interest. Our attention is often unconsciously and habitually drawn to whatever sound, sight, sensation, or thought is making the deepest impact on our mind in any moment. At other times, our attention is more conscious: we find little difficulty in giving attention to something that pleases us, such as an absorbing book, film, or conversation. Wise attention is not governed by the predominance of our senses, or by the impact of pain and pleasure. Wise attention is guided by the intention to see deeply into our life, to understand the sources of struggle and confusion, and to find the path to their end.

Our bodies, minds, and hearts are our lifelong companions; the relationship we have with them is the most intimate and enduring relationship of our life. Too often we live apart from our bodies, our emotional life is chaotic and uncertain, and our minds simply seem to have an unpredictable life of their own.

finding peace

Meditation is not a rejection of the many interests that absorb our time and attention in life. It is an acknowledgment that if we do not know how to feel at home, at ease, and at peace with ourselves, we will struggle to find ease and peace anywhere in our life. Interest, curiosity, and investigation are the key foundations of meditation practice and deep insight.

dedication and perseverance

Bearing in mind that our journey will involve peaks and valleys, highs and lows, dedication and perseverance are our path. At those moments when we are in the midst of experiences which challenge and surprise us in ways we neither expected nor wanted, dedication will keep us balanced and committed. Perseverance can also sustain us when we feel we are making no progress or are under pressure from unwanted thoughts and feelings. Instead of resigning or surrendering, our dedication and perseverance will allow us to remember why we

QUESTIONS THAT INSPIRE OUR INTEREST

1 Do we understand ourselves?

2 Do we understand the life of our hearts and minds?

3 Do we understand that struggle and confusion are optional in this life?

4 Do we understand the ways to peace, compassion, and intimacy with all things in all moments?

embarked on our journey. Dedication and perseverance allow us to stay present and open to whatever each moment brings, the welcome and the unwelcome. As such, they are essential to developing a calm attentiveness.

BE WILLING TO PERSEVERE

1 Meditation teaches us to open up to and accept each aspect of our experience. Dedication and perseverance guard us from being dissuaded or discouraged.

2 Meditation asks us not to reject, deny, or abandon anything in this life. Our willingness to persevere in all the moments we are inclined to flee is what enables us to discover the possibility of cultivating balance and peace in the midst of all things.

3 Dedication and perseverance are born of not demanding instant results or quick fixes from meditation. We cannot foresee what life will bring to us. Learning to embrace change, or not being able to control the uncontrollable in life, or grasp the ungraspable are lessons for us to deeply understand.

4 We cannot predict the future or recover the past. We can learn to find within ourselves the courage and openness to embrace life as it is, rather than demanding it conform to our expectations.

3

paths of meditation

There is no single style of meditation, a one-approach-fits-all. People come to meditation for all sorts of reasons, and approach it from many different angles. Some cultivate love and compassion; some pay more attention to their minds and bodies; others find the way forward through seeking and offering forgiveness. This chapter looks at some of the paths to meditation that people have found useful and elaborates on how they might work for you.

styles of meditation

The Buddha taught a wide spectrum of meditation styles and practices that reveal the ways of living an awakened life. These include practices of deep attentiveness, mindfulness, and insight, as well as contemplation and the cultivation of heartfelt love, joy, and compassion. These diverse practices share a clear and simple commitment—the liberation of our minds from confusion and struggle, and the cultivation of our capacity for awareness, peace, and wisdom. As you begin to meditate, you will find that it can be challenging and yet also deeply simple. Initially, these paths of meditation ask for considerable effort and application. With practice, however, they become entirely natural.

Our attitude and approach to our meditation is directly related to the realization of our aspirations. A path that holds profound peace as its goal needs to be cultivated in a spirit of peace. A path dedicated to the fulfilment of calm needs to be developed with serenity.

the possibilities

Meditation reveals both what is and what is not possible. Paths of meditation are a means to realize the understanding and compassion innate in all of us. In order to realize that potential, we need to connect fully with the truth of our life in the present. We need to learn how to be intimate with our own lives.

calming and collecting

According to the Buddha's teaching, profound wisdom and compassion are born of a calm and collected mind. Learning to bring wholehearted attention to a single point of focus serves to unify our mind and body with the present moment. A unified mind and body has an enhanced clarity and sensitivity to life. The cultivation of single-pointed attention calms the cascade of thinking that can govern our minds and lives. The point of focus provides a foundation of connection upon which serenity is developed.

points of collection

Although the point of focus changes according to the style of meditation, the aim of collecting and calming the mind remains the same. The point of focus you choose may be a sound, your breathing, or a visual object.

Endless distractedness mars our capacity to live our life fully. Learning to return to a simple point of connection rescues us from being perpetually lost in the thoughts, feelings, and images that swirl through our minds. Resistance to distracting thoughts only creates tension. Instead, we learn to gently and calmly return our attention to our chosen focus, allowing the cascade of thinking to recede naturally. With practice, we learn that we can gently return to calm and simplicity. Attention is cultivated one moment at a time.

SOME TRUTHS

It is helpful to let go of preconceptions about what meditation should feel like and what it should offer.

1 Meditation can never be a fast track to the transcendental, or seen as a quick fix for any of life's difficulties.

2 Meditation requires patience, openness, and acceptance. Each moment in our life asks for our willingness to greet it as a teacher.

3 Our path will not always be one of euphoric experiences or stunning insights. Inevitably, we will encounter moments of boredom, restlessness, and resistance.

4 Ultimately, we will learn to accept and embrace the obstacles and difficult mental states that arise as invitations to deepen our understanding.

mindfulness of breathing

The use of the breath to cultivate one-pointedness and concentration is central to the Buddha's teaching of mindfulness and insight. The ever-present nature of our breath means we always have an accessible point of focus. Mindfulness of breathing is a powerful tool on the way to developing a calm, still mind. It is a simple practice that opens the door to profound peace and insight.

The practice begins by placing our breath in the forefront of our awareness. We cultivate the intention to bring a wholehearted attention to rest within our breathing. When we learn to be intimate with our breath, we are simultaneously learning to be present in our body and to connect more fully with the moment we are living.

Countless thoughts of past and future plans, memories, and images will pass through our minds. They do not ask for resistance or judgment, but we come to understand that we are not obliged to be lost in or follow every passing thought. Learning to come back to our breath, moment to moment, is learning a life skill in letting go and simplicity.

We are learning to nurture a mind of calmness and ease, a mind of friendliness. We come to understand that the invitation to be endlessly preoccupied is one we will face

GUIDED MEDITATION: BREATHING

Adopt a relaxed and comfortable posture in which you can stand upright, but feel relaxed. Gently close your eyes.	Gently but systematically move your attention down through the whole of your body, consciously relaxing and softening any part of your body that is tense or contracted. In particular, pay attention to your hands, shoulders, and face, letting them relax and soften.	Bring your attention to rest within your breathing. Pay attention to the whole process of breathing, being aware of the life cycle of a single breath—its beginning, middle, and ending. Attend to the way that your body responds to each breath: the expanding and relaxing of your chest and abdomen, the sensation in the nostrils as you breathe in and then out.	When your mind is drawn away from your breath to thoughts or images, just simply acknowledge their presence without becoming lost in them. Be patient with your mind. In the moments you are aware your attention has wandered, simply and calmly renew your intention to connect with the next breath.

throughout our lives. We also begin to learn from experience that unsetttling or unhelpful preoccupations end with our willingness to put them down. This is their nature.

This process of attending to the breath, noticing when our attention slips away and bringing it back again and again is something that takes place over days, weeks, months, and years. It requires a gentle and patient perseverance. With practice, this will lead to the development of what is known as *samadhi*. Samadhi can best be described as a focused quality of mind that is one-pointed, unwavering, calm, and peaceful.

5 Breathe in with sensitivity, breathe out with sensitivity. Let your breath find its natural depth without forcing or controlling it in any way.

6 Attend to the pause between the ending of one out-breath and the start of the next in-breath. In that pause, rest calmly and sustain your attention within one breath and one moment at a time. Continue to rest your attention within just one breath at a time as long as you are able.

7 Continue to breathe rhythmically, then when you are ready gently open your eyes.

GUIDED MEDITATION: COUNTING AND CALMING

tip

You can substitute simple phrases for counting. As you take your in-breath, silently note it with *Breathing in calmness*, with each out-breath *Letting go, breathing out*. Use simple words that suggest the quality of mind and heart you are seeking to cultivate.

1 Adopt a posture of ease and balance, taking a moment to soften and relax your shoulders, face, neck, and hands. Close your eyes gently.

2 Focus on those points where your body makes contact with the ground. Attend to the sensations you experience in these points of contact.

3 Now breathe more fully, consciously focusing your attention within your breathing. Allow your breathing to establish a natural rhythm and depth.

4 With your first in-breath, silently count one; with the out-breath, count two. With the next, count three and so on.

5 Ensure that your counting and breathing is harmonized and coordinated.

6 Let passing thoughts that enter your mind retreat into the background in much the same way that sounds and sensations in the present moment arise and then fade.

7 Let your counting rest within the natural rhythm of your breathing. Remain present with each breath as you take it.

8 Focus on the words and your breathing simultaneously. Allow the meaning of the words combined with your focus on breathing to bring your mind and body together.

9 Moments of wandering are inevitable. The possibility of returning to simplicity and one-pointedness is no further away than the next breath. It is always possible in life and in meditation to begin anew.

10 When you feel that you are ready, you can open your eyes and come out of your posture.

OBSTACLES AND ANTIDOTES

impatience and frustration

agitation and acceptance

Prior to meditating you may find that your mind is preoccupied with a hundred different thoughts and distractions. Many conclude that this is an inappropriate moment to attempt to meditate. Rather than avoiding meditation, however, we come to understand that the moments of greatest struggle in our lives are the moments asking us to cultivate a sanctuary of inner peace.

Agitation, unrest, and turmoil are not obstacles to meditation. The obstacle lies in our desire to distract and divert ourselves when we feel restless or uneasy. A path of wisdom teaches us to engage with our chaotic, confused, and conflicted minds as the place we learn to find genuine calm and balance. Acceptance is a crucial element in transformation: learning to see life as it is rather than as we demand it should be. Every moment of confusion, difficulty, or pain is a gateway to learning the ways to cultivate calm and understanding. At these moments we discover, through calm attentiveness, to cultivate simplicity within chaos. We cannot control all of the agitation we meet in life; we can learn to calm the agitation within our own hearts.

frustration and patience

As you develop your path, you may have feelings of frustration and impatience that feel like obstacles to your meditation. These are exactly the same as those feelings that mar our capacity to live our life wholeheartedly. These feelings do not ask for condemnation or resistance but for a compassionate, gentle perseverance in accepting their presence.

Investigate these feelings of frustration as you experience them. Ask yourself: *How does this feel?*; *Where do I experience it in my body?*; and *What effect is it having upon me?* Include your frustration in the focus of your attention. Our life and meditation ask for a depth of patience that does not always feel accessible to us. We can always begin again in our life, knowing that patience is a quality that allows us to find a sense of ease within the difficult.

visualization

Visualization is another widely practiced style of meditation that can help us to develop our capacity for simple and clear attentiveness. An image, color, or symbolic object can all be used as objects of attention for you to focus upon. Ultimately, visualization helps us to integrate our minds with our bodies.

Begin by placing a picture or object in front of you, then gently focus your attention on the object to establish a visual connection. Once you have the image firmly in your mind's eye, close your eyes and attempt to recall the image in your mind. Begin by reconstructing the image with each individually remembered element, color, and shape. Open your eyes and reestablish your visual connection to the object.

As you continue this process of establishing a visual connection and then recalling it, you will notice that

GUIDED MEDITATION: VISUALIZATION

1	Adopt a relaxed and upright posture.
2	Place your chosen object in front of you and bring your eyes to rest on it. Relax your mind and body as you focus on the object. Explore the object with your attention.
3	Once you feel connected with your object, close your eyes and sustain the image of the object in your mind's eye. If the image is partial or too vague to begin with, begin reconstructing it element-by-element, sensing what you do remember of the image.
4	When this image becomes vague, open your eyes and look again at the object in front of you. Once you have reestablished your connection with the image, close your eyes once more and sustain the image in your mind.
5	Allow your attention to become fully focused on the image and sustain it in your mind for as long as possible.
6	Thoughts, sensations, and images will continue to arise. Let them pass without becoming preoccupied with them.
7	Allow the deepening sense of inner spaciousness and calm to spread to your mind and body. You will feel your restlessness and agitation recede.
8	When ready, open your eyes and come out of the posture.

you are finding this is done with greater ease and clarity. Eventually, all exterior thoughts and feelings will start to recede and the symbol absorbs your attention fully.

choice of object

There are many objects that are suitable for your attention. Choose something from the natural world, such as a pebble or flower, or you could pick a beautifully colored candle.

dullness and alertness

We may find when we attempt to focus that we become dull or sleepy. These are entirely natural states and may be the product of stress, lack of sleep, exhaustion, or resistance.

Simple adjustments can help to lift dullness. Experiment with meditating with your eyes open. Check that your posture is alert and upright. You could also try meditating while standing up. Ultimately, this too is a transitory state. Gentle perseverance and the clear intention to be as awake as possible will alleviate dullness.

restlessness and calm

Restlessness is part of our lives born of feeling ill at ease within our minds, bodies, and the moment we are living.

The impulse in our life and meditation is to move, to find something more gratifying to engage in. Restlessness, too, is just a passing sensation. Recognizing this, we find we can hold it gently in our attention, much like any of the other sensations we experience. We find that we are able to commit ourselves to stillness. Restlessness often proves to be merely a habit of mind and life, which prompts us to lean forward constantly into the next moment.

Contentment and ease are rare blessings in our life. They are not simply accidents but born of learning how and where to find the richness and depth within all the small moments of our life.

AN ANTIDOTE TO RESTLESSNESS

1 Learning to calm and still our mind and body is the antidote to restlessness.

2 Ensure your posture is one that really allows you to relax and be still.

3 When experiencing restlessness, experiment with different postures to find what suits you best. Bring an intentional relaxation and calm to your posture.

4 Bring a conscious attention to those parts of your body that feel tense and allow them to soften.

5 Find an object of attention in the moment you can clearly attend to, whether your breathing, body, or listening.

dullness and alertness continued

We live in a world of sound. Some sounds are welcome and delightful, while others we experience as disturbing and irritating. Often we wish that there was a way to end the intrusion of these sounds into our lives, so we avoid or resist them. But this ongoing resistance serves only to make us defensive and aversive. Through learning to cultivate wise attention in places of resistance, we come to understand that irritation and aversion lie not in the sounds, but in our hearts and minds. Eventually, we understand that sound has no innate power to shatter inner peace.

embracing sound

Listening meditation allows us to befriend sound and abandon our judgments of what constitutes noise. Instead we embrace the spectrum of sounds that we find in our daily life, enhancing our capacity for sensitivity and attention. Listening with sensitivity, we come to understand that sound in all its forms constitutes the sound of life itself. Rather than becoming overwhelmed and upset, we discover the possibility of remaining calm and centered amid the spectrum of sounds that are part of our life. Genuine calmness is incompatible with blocking out any aspect of the world around us. Profound calm rests on our willingness to embrace every aspect of our life, inwardly and outwardly.

LISTENING WITH SENSITIVITY

1 Adopt an alert and calm posture.

2 Soften your body, close your eyes, and fully relax, softening your body.

3 Now bring your attention to listening, being aware of those sounds that are present in the moment.

4 Notice the sounds that are distant and those that are close to you.

5 Listen to the sounds carefully and sense where they begin and end, noting their changes in both tone and intensity.

6 Sense, but do not resist, those moments when your attention shifts from simply listening to judging, describing, and categorizing. Now gradually let go of these interpretations and bring your mind back to simply listening attentively.

7 Be attentive to the moments when you either respond to or recoil from sounds that you welcome or resist. Attend to each sound in turn, whether pleasant or unpleasant. Bring the same sensitivity and receptivity to sounds you dislike, as you to those you like.

8 When you find thoughts becoming the focus of your attention, let them pass and recede. By just listening, stay as fully present as possible.

9 Be attentive to the variations in sounds, their rhythms, and the way in which they arrive and then recede. Focus on the moments of silence that occur, however briefly, between sounds.

10 When a moment of silence arrives, rest within it. Continue listening until you feel ready, then open your eyes and come out of the posture.

body awareness

We rarely attend to the life of our bodies, unless we have to because of illness or pain. The Buddha taught that everything we are asked to learn in this life can be learned within the life of our bodies. By being present within our bodies, we find an enhanced ability to attend to the whole of our life with mindfulness. By learning to understand and treat our own bodies with greater sensitivity, we bring greater understanding to every one of our relationships.

Listening to the life of our bodies is to refine our ability to recognize those moments when we slip from calm to agitation. By exploring the range of pleasurable, neutral, and painful sensations that we experience on a moment-to-moment basis, we are better able to relate to these changes in every area of our lives.

fear of pain

Habit often forces us to fear the painful and seek the pleasurable. By fearing pain, we necessarily live a life that is circumscribed by it as we try and avoid, suppress, and ignore it. Listening to our bodies with sensitivity allows us to avoid the states of unconscious reaction, and teaches us the nature of mortality, change, acceptance, and the need to let go. We also discover that our attempts to control, judge, and coerce our feelings are counterproductive. Most

important, the impossibility of controlling life becomes clear.

As we learn we can find a greater equanimity with the range of sensations that our bodies experience, we are increasingly able to abandon our old preconceptions of what constitutes pain, pleasure, or neutral feelings. Our minds become calmer, clearer, and happier as we no longer respond to sensation with our habitual impulses to preserve or to reject different sensations.

Instead, the body here acts as a metaphor and template for the rest of our lives. In the same way that we find balance within the changing sensations and experiences of our bodies, so we are able to accept and embrace the changing sensations and experiences that life brings. We begin to become conscious of the liberating and life-enhancing possibility of freeing ourselves from struggle and resistance.

GUIDED MEDITATION: THE BODY

1 Adopt a relaxed and alert posture. Close your eyes gently. Bring the focus of your attention into your body.

2 With each in-breath and out-breath, pay attention to the rising and falling of your abdomen. Focus on this rhythm to steady your attention. When you find your focus wavering, gently return it to your breathing.

3 Focus your attention on the top of your head, alert to any sensations present there. Now expand your focus of attention, slowly moving it down over your face, paying attention to where you feel sensation and equally to the places where there is no sensation.

4 Continue to move your focus down through your neck, chest, and shoulders. Continue this calm, sensitive movement of attention down through both of your arms and into your hands. As you do this, pay attention to the range of sensations that your body is constantly relaying to you—the neutral, the unpleasant, and the pleasant.

5 When you start to resist a difficult or unpleasant sensation in your body, bring a gentle attentiveness to that part of your body instead of avoiding it. Equally, when you sense neutral feelings and areas that lack sensation, embrace and accept them as they are, and attend to them as equally as you do those that are pleasant and unpleasant.

6 Begin an exploration of your chest, stomach, and lower body. Notice the way that different sensations appear and then fade away. Some of these sensations will be strong and obvious, while others more subtle and difficult to perceive. Attend equally to the entire range of sensations you detect in your body.

7 Keep moving the flow of your attention down through your body toward your legs and into your feet. As you experience moments where you are drawn into thought, gently return your attention to your body.

8 As you feel your focus arrive in your feet and at the tips of your toes, gently begin to move it back up through your body, reversing the process. When you feel you want to hurry, judge, or become distracted, simply return your focus back to the life of your body.

9 Let go of any preconceptions or preferences about what kind of sensations may arise. Inner balance and equanimity are born of cultivating an equality of attentiveness to all things.

10 Continue to systematically move your attention through your body for the duration of the meditation, attending from moment to moment to each of the signals and messages that your body gives you. When you feel ready, relax your posture, rest for a moment and then open your eyes.

obstacles to awareness

There are many obstacles to developing an awareness of the body, but once these are recognized, they become easier to handle.

fear, aversion, and resistance

Perhaps the most debilitating and paralyzing of emotions in our lives is fear. Fear lies at the heart of many of our most difficult emotional experiences. Fear can also be hard to recognize for what it is.

■ Fear can range from small anxious pangs through to overwhelming waves of dread and terror.

■ All fear prevents us from embracing our life experiences with openness and clarity.

■ Fear may also take on the form of mistrust, self-doubt, and self-consciousness.

■ One of our greatest fears is the fear of pain.

reactions to pain

Our first choice when we encounter fear is to resist, ignore, or retreat from it. We are conditioned to react to fear with various strategies that avoid it or camouflage it with distraction. When meditating, we invite ourselves to turn directly toward fear and anxiety and, in time, this allows us to embrace fear

with a loving and compassionate attention. Resistance to being with ourselves is a predominant expression of fear. Yet we discover that when we cannot be at home within our own minds, hearts, and bodies, we rarely feel at ease anywhere in the world. Consistently avoiding fear is to give it permission to govern our lives. Learning to investigate and understand our fears is to diminish that power..

meeting with pain and fear

When we experience pain, our learned response is to try and distance ourselves from it through distraction, flight, or explanation. Pain takes a firmer grip of our consciousness in our apprehension of how it will continue or magnify. These conditioned fearful reactions to pain serve to undermine a skillful and organic reaction to the reality of the moments of pain that will touch all of our lives, and erode our confidence in our capacity to meet pain with compassion and equanimity.

■ Meditation offers us a radically different way of responding to pain, both physical pain, and general pain in life.

■ In much the same way that meditation is able to transform our understanding and response to fear, so is it able to change the ways in which we respond to pain.

- Instead of simply resorting to conditioned responses of resistance and distress, we learn to investigate with calm and genuine curiosity what we are experiencing.

- Resistance and aversion are replaced with a gentle, compassionate, and accepting attention of pain.

accepting pain

When we investigate the landscape of our pain, we recognize that in trying to avoid it or resist it we make it worse. By bringing a compassionate and accepting attention to pain, we substantively change the way in which we experience it. We discover that pain is not the solid mass of sensation that we previously assumed. We begin to realize that the sensation of pain is changing from moment to moment.

As we begin to accept pain, we notice that there are a multitude of textures present within the sensation that we identify as "pain." We also notice that in all types of pain and distress there are two distinct tiers to what we experience. The first is the actuality of the sensation itself, and the second is the conditioned fear that surrounds it.

By letting go of this conditioned fear, we find we are able to connect with the simple truth of the sensation and in doing so, we can find the calm and balance to accept it.

MEDITATION: MEETING PAIN WITH EQUANIMITY

1 Adopt an alert posture that allows you to be relaxed and at ease. Close your eyes gently. For a moment, just be aware of your entire body. Consciously relax those points on your body that are tight or tense. Allow your face, jaw, shoulders, and hands to gently soften and relax.

2 Be aware of those points on your body that make contact with the floor. Sense the pressure and sensation arising from those points of contact.

3 Expand your attention to be aware of your entire body, letting go of ideas you may have about how you ought to be feeling. Bring a compassionate and wholehearted attention to your body as it is in this moment.

4 Allow your attention to include the pain or discomfort you are experiencing. Attend from moment to moment to each signal and message that your body gives you. Pay attention as you map the landscape of areas of pain. Notice how pain is a changing mass of sensations. Experience its ebb and flow as it arrives and subsides.

5 If the pain intensifies, take your attention to a place in your body that is either neutral or more pleasant—the palms of your hands or the touch of your lips together. Sense the falling away of resistance as you focus here, then return your attention to the area of pain, bringing the same ease and willingness to be present.

6 Attend equally to the entire range of sensations you detect in your body, the strong and the subtle, the pleasurable and the painful.

7 Rest with this quality of awareness for as long as feels appropriate for you at this time. When you feel ready relax your posture, rest for a moment and then open your eyes.

the nature of our minds

The Buddha taught that the mind is the forerunner of all things. Our speech, actions, choices, and the way we interpret the world originate in our mind. Sometimes our mind can be a place of serenity, stillness, clarity, and calm. Often it appears to be a tangled web of thoughts, regrets, worries, and changing anxieties. By understanding the nature of our mind, we will find that we are able to inhabit a mental landscape of clarity and calm.

Central to understanding our mind better is the ability to approach the thoughts and feelings that emerge from it with interest and mindfulness.

To understand and transform our minds is to transform our life. We become aware of the arising and passing of thoughts, images, and mental states on a moment-to-moment level. Rather than being an obstacle to deep understanding and compassion, our minds are the best and only means to achieving a life of calm, compassion, and wisdom.

being intimate with your mind

Clarity of mind comes when we stop blaming our minds and instead approach them with interest, investigation, and sensitivity.

The mind is capable of being both creative and destructive. A clearer understanding of our minds enables us to approach the challenges we encounter with greater creativity. As our thinking becomes less polarized, we will be better able to meet with sensitivity and insight the divergent views and ideas in the world. By recognizing the ability of our mind to produce both confusion and chaos and great joy and clarity, we learn to bring a mindful awareness to the range of thoughts that we experience. In doing so, we see that a thought is just a thought, subject to the same rising and passing as any other sensation, image, and feeling in our lives.

enhancing thinking

Meditation is not a means to suppress "thinking." A calm mind is not without thought, but one in which we are able to investigate our thoughts in a non-judgmental, compassionate, and calm way. When we do this, we improve our capacity to think and reflect with clarity. Inner simplicity is born of willingness to learn how to let go.

By looking at our minds on a moment-to-moment level, we begin to better understand the direct and very real relationship between our state of mind and our body. Meditation is fundamentally about listening without prejudice to our minds. The liberation of being able to listen to our minds without rejecting, interpreting, or judging brings clarity and calm.

When we understand our mind on a moment-to-moment level, we begin to explore its movements and activities, and realize that the mind is involved in an endless series of rising and passing thoughts, images, memories, moods, and responses. We become more aware of the way our associations, memories, and emotions shape our conclusions. Through introducing the qualities of investigation, serenity, and simplicity into our minds, we discover we are not sentenced to helplessness in the face of thought and emotion. Seeing how our mind shapes our experience of life moment to moment, we are able to cultivate the clarity and calmness that profoundly impact our life.

the power of mood

Each response that we give in life is shaped and formed by the state of our mind. Our thoughts, words, and responses are to some extent always governed by our mental states and moods. By reflecting on a typical day and the changing way in which you respond to the events and thoughts that occur, we begin to sense the power of our moods and mental states. When we are agitated, we are prone to react to the world with agitation. Thoughts and words of kindness and compassion are rarely the products of an aversive mind.

Meditation is about understanding the impact of these mental states, and learning to cultivate what is beneficial, and release the mental states that undermine well-being.

THOUGHT IN THE MOMENT

1 Thought is a multilayered process. Sometimes our thoughts are fleeting and random; in other moments, they can be elaborate and time-consuming fantasies and obsessions.

2 Too often thought is used to comfort and distract ourselves from a life we find difficult to bear. Yet this kind of thinking rarely brings the ease we long for. Instead it deepens resentment as we notice the disparity between our fantasies and the reality we inhabit. Mentally constructed worlds of unrealistic expectation disconnect us from the moment.

3 At other times, we suffer insistent and repetitive thoughts that consume all sense of spaciousness. We find ourselves anxious about the future and replaying the past in countless moments. When this happens, our confidence in finding clarity and calm seems more remote than ever.

4 Nurturing our capacity to reflect, to inquire, and to investigate thought can bring a new level of understanding into our lives.

5 We can learn to see a thought as a thought, arising and passing in the same way as all things in our life.

your state of mind

MEDITATION: EXPERIENCING YOUR MIND

1 Adopt a posture that is both calm and relaxed. Gently allow your eyes to close. Bring your attention to your breathing and establish your attention inwardly and in the moment.

2 Be aware of your body and any points of tension that you can detect. Consciously soften and relax your body. Let any thoughts of past or future, or preoccupations with the present recede to the back of your mind. Bring your attention to the present, where you are, in this moment.

3 Try to sense what your state of mind is at this moment. Do you feel agitated, upset, vulnerable, happy, generous, pessimistic, or content? Now turn your attention to your body. Be aware of how your state of mind may be mirrored in your body in tension, restlessness, or pain. Explore whether it is possible to soften all of those places.

4 If you sense an underlying state of mind, ask yourself what it needs. In the face of agitation, cultivate spacious attention, be aware of the stillness of your body and turn your attention to listening. In the face of preoccupation or obsession, explore if it is possible to rest your attention more clearly within just one breath at a time, renewing your intention to let go. Clearly sense the pause between the ending of an out-breath and the beginning of an in-breath.

5 At those moments when you feel that you are in the grip of resentment, fear, and anger, ask yourself what you need to cultivate to restore balance, responsiveness, and openness.

6 As your awareness of your state of mind emerges, try to be fully awake and present with that state of mind with acceptance and kindness. Recognize the impermanence of all mental states.

7 Sense the different states of mind that emerge and then recede within your mind throughout the course of your meditation.

8 When you feel ready, open your eyes and come out of your posture.

MEDITATION: INVESTIGATING THE MIND

1 Adopt an upright, alert, and relaxed posture.

2 Close your eyes gently.

3 Bring your attention to your breathing, sensing each in-breath and out-breath. Attend to the wider sensations present in your body. Be aware of the way in which each sensation arises in the body and then passes.

4 Now bring your attention to the whole of your body. Allow yourself to settle deeply into a stillness and bodily awareness.

5 Now be aware of your mind as it is in this moment. Allow yourself to be aware of the range of thoughts that arise and then subside without dwelling on any of them.

6 Be aware of the way in which thoughts and images are temporary and passing mental events that are constantly emerging, subsiding, and then being replaced. Sense those images that you feel linger longer in your consciousness and how you respond to them.

7 Bring a calm questioning response to these thoughts that persist. Ask yourself: *What is this?* Do not look for an easy or instant answer to this question, but rather keep asking it about the thoughts and images that arise.

8 Let the question *What is this?* be the anchor for your attention, allowing you to see your thoughts as they really are.

9 Avoid posing the question in an overly mechanical way. Each time you pose the question make it a genuine inquiry into each moment.

10 If your mind digresses or wanders, simply repeat the question, investigating this new direction in your thinking. Do not resist the diversion but instead seek to understand it for what it is.

obstacles to an open mind

Love, compassion, generosity, and joy all originate within our hearts. If we are to experience any of these to their fullest, then we need to live with an awakened and open heart. All of us will experience moments of hardship and heartbreak. Yet the extent to which we respond to them rests on the wisdom of our heart.

living with an open heart

A wise heart allows us to love, care, and commit to the qualities of compassion, generosity, and forgiveness. The pain and anguish we meet are healed by these qualities.

A universal characteristic shared by all human beings is the capacity to hurt and be hurt. At times, it seems easier to be angry than kind, to harbor resentment rather than offer forgiveness, to blame rather than to be patient, and to fear rather than love. Insult, humiliation, dismissal, and rejection are unavoidable in life, yet they do not need to dominate our lives. Hatred and compassion deepen through the attention we give to them.

We often spend more time thinking about people we hate rather than those we love. We can obsess incessantly about those who have harmed us while they have forgotten and moved on in their lives.

When we live our lives immersed in feelings of regret and bitterness, we are forfeiting life in the moment. The heart then becomes a prison as resentment and fear begin to govern every aspect of

our lives. Pain always comes from without, but it is only possible for healing to come from within.

learning to forgive

We may also find it difficult to forgive ourselves. When we harm another, guilt, regret, and remorse overtake us. Life is lived in the past, the phrases "if only" and "I wish" dominate our consciousness. Often we find it difficult to reconcile with those we have hurt, because we sense the divide of mistrust and anger that our words and actions have created.

When we feel resistant to forgiveness, we should remember that the alternative is carrying around this hurt. Forgiveness offers a life free from the burdens of the painful past. In finding a present that is not ruled by the past, we find peace and the ability to live with openness and trust.

turning toward others

Forgiveness is rooted in the principles of tolerance, acceptance, and compassion, applied equally to ourselves and others. Forgiveness asks us to turn toward those we avoid or fear. It also demands that we look with clarity at the nature of our hurt and any hurt that we may have caused. In doing this, we become aware of a very simple choice that forgiveness extends to us: we can linger in the pain of the past or choose to meet it with understanding, compassion, and courage, and live in the present.

LETTING GO

1 Perhaps our greatest obstacle to understanding the life of our minds is our tendency to cling to ideas, thoughts, and feelings. Endless replays of the past, stories of resentment or guilt, and rehearsals of the future repeat themselves in our minds.

2 Such clinging and holding inhibit our capacity for spaciousness and our ability to live fully the moment we are in. Learning to let go of these obsessions, in each moment, is in itself the ability to find balance and serenity.

3 Anxiety and confusion lead us to cling to one thing after another, inwardly and outwardly. Letting go is not the product of force or willpower, but is rooted in calm, compassion, and understanding.

4 Each time we meditate, we need to be ready to let go of the thoughts, memories, and images that appear, just as life continues to ask us to let go in countless ways.

5 Meditation enables us to bring a wholehearted attention to those moments in our lives where we feel most troubled and where our states of mind bind us and create sorrow. The source of our greatest unhappiness is often those opinions, expectations, roles, identities, and desires that we cling and hold onto. The more that we learn to let go, the more generosity, compassion, simplicity, and freedom we have in our lives.

forgiving yourself

MEDITATION: FINDING FORGIVENESS FOR OURSELVES

1 Spend a moment settling into a calm and easy posture. Rest your attention in the center of your chest, in your heart, allowing sensitivity and attention to emerge.

2 Now sense the hurt or pain you may have inflicted on yourself in the past through your thoughts, words, or actions. Sense the regrets you feel for any way you have hurt another through your own thoughts, words, or actions.

3 As these memories come back to you, accept each image, bodily feeling, and thought without rejecting or judging those moments, even if they are deeply painful. Sense what it would be to let go of the guilt, anxiety, or self-judging that is rooted in the past. Sense what you feel forgiveness means in this moment. Ask yourself what it might mean to release the burden of the past and your regrets relating to it.

4 While repeating these phrases, rest your attention within your heart: *I forgive myself. I forgive myself for the hurt I have done to myself through fear, pain, and confusion. I forgive myself for those thoughts, words, and actions that have done me harm. I forgive myself for the harm or hurt I have consciously or unconsciously inflicted on another.*

5 Keep repeating these phrases for several minutes. Allow your attention to fully rest within the words and sense the freedom implicit within them. As you repeat the phrases, reflect on the possibility of fully letting go of the past.

6 As memories and thoughts that bring guilt, resentment, and regret arise, allow them to pass and return your attention to the center of your chest within your forgiving heart. When you feel ready, slowly open your eyes and come out of your posture.

forgiveness from others

MEDITATION: ASKING FOR FORGIVENESS

In our lives, we will inevitably cause hurt to others out of confusion, fear, and pain. We don't always understand the impact that our words and actions have upon another person. Remorse and guilt are the burden born of habitual fear and anger. By asking others for forgiveness, we free ourselves to be sensitive, honest, and compassionate in the present.

1 Assume a posture of ease and balance, gently closing your eyes.

2 As you breathe out, release agitation and chaos within your mind.

3 Allow the emotions, images, and memories of the times when you hurt others to arise in your mind. Sense the sorrow you feel for any way you may have harmed another person, intentionally or unintentionally. As the many different situations and people come to mind, make room for each and everyone of them.

4 Sense what it would be like to release yourself from this burden. Allow yourself to feel the wounds of your regret slowly begin to heal.

5 Move your attention to those from whom you are asking forgiveness. Invite those people into your heart and attention.

6 Allow them to sit with you in your meditation and share with them the following phrases.

7 *I ask your forgiveness for any way in which I have caused you pain or hurt.*

I ask your forgiveness for any way in which I have neglected you.

I ask your forgiveness for any way in which I have made you fear me.

8 Rest your attention in those phrases for a moment. Keeping your focus in the present, let go of past regret as you make a commitment to kindness and openness of heart in the present.

9 Once you feel ready, open your eyes and relax your posture.

forgiveness for those who cause pain

It is challenging to forgive those who have caused suffering to us and those around us. Rather than blame, compassion asks us to understand and forgive the anger, fear, and confusion that causes people to act in this way. Compassion and forgiveness cannot be separated from understanding. When someone hurts us, we feel alienated from them. Yet forgiveness is intimate, crossing the abyss of separation. Forgiveness is neither the surrender of discriminating wisdom nor the condoning of any act of harm. It is concerned with the healing of what can be healed and cultivating the empathy that allows us to understand the power of fear to inflict harm.

generosity and compassion

Forgiveness requires a generosity that can seem elusive. The simple act of approaching those who have hurt us can seem insurmountable. It requires balance and courage to engage those who have hurt us with forgiveness. Sometimes we inch toward forgiveness.

The forgiveness we extend to others is an act of compassion for ourselves. We are freed to live our lives fully, no longer burdened by the fear and anger that dominated us. By forgiving, we lift ourselves out of the world of blame, anger, and hatred. When we forgive others, we are forgiving the forces of confusion, ignorance, fear, and anger that we all encounter during our lives.

MEDITATION: FORGIVENESS FOR THOSE WHO CAUSE US PAIN

1 Assume a posture that is relaxed and free from tension.

2 Close your eyes gently and allow your body to soften.

3 Sensing your heart in the center of your chest, bring a calm and gentle attention to rest there.

4 Allow into your attention someone who has hurt you. This could be a small slight you have been unable to forget or a hurt that has followed you through your life.

5 Focus on this person and sense the range of feelings and thoughts that arise without judging any of them. Make room in your heart for rage, sadness, fear, and mistrust.

6 Focusing on the pain that you are carrying with you from the past, sense that the time has come to free yourself from this burden.

7 As you keep your focus on the person you felt has hurt you, gently begin to offer the intention of forgiveness.

8 Repeat these phrases:

I forgive you for the pain you have caused in my life.

I forgive you for the pain you have caused me due to the anger, confusion, and ignorance in your heart.

I offer you forgiveness for the hurt you caused me.

9 Rest your attention in the phrases and intentions of forgiveness. Be alive to those moments when you feel a small opening or opportunity of forgiveness and compassion. Sense the opportunity for a new beginning and feel the weight of past hurt lifted from you.

10 You may struggle to stay engaged with the image and memory of someone who hurt you so much. If you feel the memory is too painful, allow your attention to retreat to your body and breathing. Soften and relax your body and, when you feel ready, return to the phrases.

11 When you feel ready, open your eyes and relax your posture.

compassion and suffering

Compassion is a response to pain, suffering, and anguish. A compassionate heart refuses to make a hierarchy of pain, but listens to the many sorrows in the world. Compassion is neither a denial of suffering nor an end to it, but a means by which to bring a receptive and honest empathy to pain and hurt. Compassion is a commitment to ending and healing the causes of suffering.

The Buddha likened wisdom and compassion to the two wings of a bird—intrinsically interwoven. If we are to develop a wise path, we must also develop a compassionate one. Wisdom reveals that life contains suffering and sorrow, and compassion is needed wherever they occur. Wisdom reveals that suffering is not an enemy. Compassion helps us to heal sorrow.

When we are struggling with grief, loss, and hurt, it is the compassionate, receptive presence of another that touches our hearts. A broken heart does not seek solutions or answers but listens with empathy and kindness. Each one of us will meet our measure of sorrow in life and will be healed by compassion.

We often feel powerless in the face of pain. Our sorrow can seem an overwhelming wave that threatens to submerge us. We need to recognize that compassion begins in the moment we find the courage to embrace pain. When we awaken our hearts, we are able to find the balance and calm necessary to accept the sorrow the world brings without it destroying us.

These are moments of powerful connection and healing.

UNDERSTANDING COMPASSION

1 Compassion asks us to find the willingness to listen to the anguish of the world around us. Wisdom teaches us that we endanger ourselves by turning away from pain and its causes.

2 Compassion also recognizes that sometimes suffering in this world is essentially blameless. There is not always a solution for broken hearts, a terminal illness, an unexpected bereavement, mental illness, or any other seemingly inexplicable calamity that can befall any of us.

3 Compassion acknowledges this, setting aside the pathways of blame, judgment, and control, and cultivating the pathways of empathy, equanimity, and courage.

4 Compassion allows us to be awake and receptive to this pain without being overwhelmed. We have all had moments in our life, both big and small, where we have responded with compassion to suffering we have witnessed. When this happens, we become indivisible from those we extend compassion to, joining that person in the moment and seeing ourselves in the eyes of another person.

MEDITATION: COMPASSION IN THE FACE OF SORROW

1 Assume a relaxed and comfortable posture.

2 Gently close your eyes. Bring your attention to the stillness and life within your body.

3 Now move your attention to the center of your chest and allow it to settle in your heart. For a few moments, bring your focus onto your breathing, sensing each in-breath and out-breath.

4 Allow your mind to settle into a relaxed and calm state.

5 Invite into your heart your awareness of another's suffering. It may be someone close to you or a situation of deep anguish that has touched your heart. Allow yourself to feel the struggle and sorrow of this situation and those who are caught up in it. For a moment, reflect on the nature of their pain and what they are experiencing.

6 Offer your empathy and sensitivity to those in that situation. Extend your heartfelt wishes for their healing. *May you find peace. May you find healing.*

7 Let these phrases become the focus of your attention for a few moments; allow them to rest in your heart and attention. You may find yourself lost in sorrow, pity, or anxiety. When this occurs, bring yourself back to your breathing, allowing yourself a moment to center yourself.

8 Choose words and phrases that are appropriate to the situation and people you are thinking about. As you repeat each phrase, stay with it for as long as you feel is appropriate.

9 It may be that you are the one most in need of compassion. In the face of struggle and sorrow, we too need to learn to extend that same empathy, generosity, and compassion to ourselves.

10 Offer to yourself the same heartfelt wishes for your own healing: *May I find peace. May I find healing.*

11 Before ending, extend those same intentions to all living things: *May all beings find peace and healing.*

loving kindness

We all long to receive acceptance, generosity, friendliness, and warmth from those who surround us and to live with kindness. Loving kindness is concerned with the unconditional warmth and care that we are capable of extending to those who are part of our lives, those we are very close to, those we are indifferent to, the people we struggle with, and ourselves. By bringing loving kindness to bear on those who we are indifferent to or alienated from, we discover that mistrust and fear are optional experiences. In the process of developing loving kindness, we develop fearlessness, tenderness, and benevolence, leading to a life of connectedness and calm. Small gestures can be powerful, and the warmth extended in a simple loving act or word has the capacity to heal and touch the heart of another. Loving kindness wakens our hearts and can change our world.

the absence of kindness

We have all experienced the harm that anger, fear, and hate can bring in our lives. Each day brings us news of yet more atrocities, hatred, and violence, scarring the lives of countless individuals. There can never be too much loving kindness; there is often too little.

Like all living sentient beings, we share a desire to be free from pain, fear, and unhappiness. We all want to be accepted, loved, and cared for. When we encounter rage, we tend to retreat and recoil from that person or situation, or retaliate with anger. Anger and fear blind our hearts.

EMBRACING LOVING KINDNESS

When we develop loving kindness, we are seeking a refuge within our hearts that is trustworthy and calm. Loving kindness can protect us from fear, anger, and turmoil. With loving kindness meditation, we remember, honor, and develop the capacity we have to lessen the mountain of suffering and alienation in our world.

When we undertake loving kindness meditation, we are developing our ability to embrace all moments with generosity and warmth. By developing our capacity for intimacy and understanding, we make more real the prospect of happiness. In essence, loving kindness meditation is a practice of happiness.

We begin practicing loving kindness with the person that many find it most difficult to extend to, namely ourselves. Many find it is easier to love and care for others than to offer these same qualities to themselves. Sometimes our lives seem to have conspired to make us feel worthless, undeserving of love or care. Loving kindness undoes this belief and replaces it with a boundless generosity, acceptance, and tenderness for who we are.

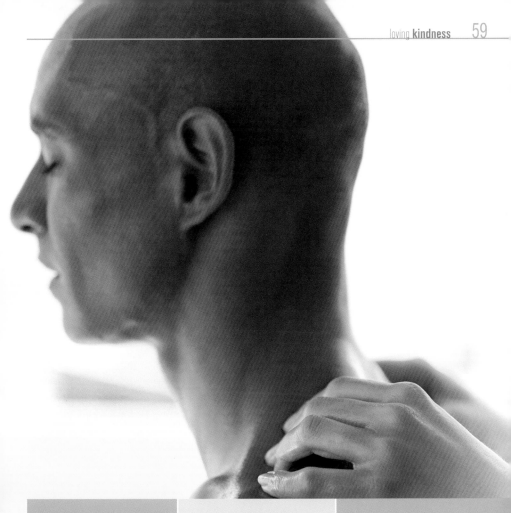

Cultivating loving kindness for ourselves, we need to let go of the painful demands, expectations, and judgements that we have acquired through our lives. Learning how to bring patience, attentiveness, tolerance, and warmth to ourselves is to learn to bring those same qualities to all of our relationships.

4

We develop loving kindness by establishing our attention with a few simple phrases that embody our intentions for happiness and well-being. Using these phrases, we trust that our lives can be a place of fearlessness, warmth, and balance.

5

Loving kindness is a path developed in formal meditation practice, as well as cultivated in all moments of our lives. Ill will is painful, whereas friendliness is peace making.

6

loving kindness continued

LOVING KINDNESS FOR YOURSELF

1 Assume a position that is both relaxed and also comfortable.

2 Bring your focus onto your breathing, sensing each in-breath and each out-breath.

3 Bring your focus to rest in your heart at the center of your chest.

4 Silently offer to yourself the intentions of loving kindness, while sensing the meaning of each of these phrases.

5 *May I be peaceful. May I be happy.*
May I be safe and protected.

6 Allow each phrase to rest gently in your heart and mind, offering to yourself your heartfelt wishes for your own well-being and happiness.

7 Sense the potential for pain and well-being that exist within your body. Bring your attention onto your body and continue to rest your attention in the following phrases.

8 *May I be peaceful.*
May I be happy.
May I be safe and protected.

9 Become aware of the life of your mind and the range of emotions it can experience. Sense the confusion, stillness, spaciousness, contractedness, serenity, and calm that the mind can bring. As you do so, gently repeat the following phrases.

10 *May I be peaceful. May I be happy.*
May I be safe and protected.

11 Become aware of the life of your heart and all the joy and sorrow that you can experience. With loving kindness, embrace anger, fear, love, trust, and happiness with calm, wisdom, and serenity.

12 Continue to focus your attention within the phrases.

13 You may find that long-submerged feelings of anger, pain, or confusion come to the surface. Understand that they too can be received with loving kindness and befriended.

14 Extend the circle of your loving kindness to a benefactor, a good friend, a person you feel indifferent toward, one by one. To each, offer your heartfelt wishes for their well-being.

15 *May you be peaceful. May you be happy.*
May you be safe and protected.

16 When you feel ready, you may open your eyes and come out of the posture.

4

daily meditation

Meditation is applicable to every daily activity, from the moment you awake until you close your eyes to sleep. There is no activity that cannot form the focus for meditation; in fact, challenging habit through meditation can help your practice. This chapter looks at meditation when walking and eating, speaking and listening, the benefits of challenging habits in daily life, and how to cultivate simplicity in your life.

meditation in every moment

The path of meditation is intended to illuminate and awaken every area of our life, both inwardly and outwardly. In the silence and solitude of formal meditation, we learn to cultivate and nurture inner stillness, calm, attentiveness, and sensitivity. Yet our practice and cultivation would be of limited value if we then entered into our life forsaking the understanding and depth we have nurtured for the more familiar territory of habit, restlessness, and anxiety. The reality is that meditation is a path we are invited to integrate into each moment of our life and holds the potential to transform our day-to-day existence. Our life is radically changed by the mindfulness, compassion, and balance we bring to the myriad of encounters that each day presents. The Buddha encouraged the living of a meditative life, in which mindfulness permeates our speech, work, relationships, and all the choices we make. We cannot choose to disengage from the world we are part of. Wisdom teaches us that we can choose how we engage with that world.

MEDITATION: ENGAGING WITH THE WORLD

In countless monasteries in Asia, monks and nuns spend their days not only in solitude and formal meditation, but also attending to the care of their communities, and engaging in the countless tasks that all of our lives present. An abbot in a monastery listened to a student who begrudged the time involved in these tasks and complained of the endless noise of the monastery, saying "How can I be expected to meditate in the midst of all of this?" The abbot answered, "How can you not?" The vast majority of those who undertake a meditative path neither intend to withdraw to a monastery or retreat from daily life, nor do they have an idealized perfect lifestyle, free of demands and responsibilities.

1. A meditative life does not demand our withdrawal from the world but our willingness to bring the monastery into our life with all of its commitments, challenges, and engagement.

2. We learn to bring into all the moments of our life, with all their imperfections, a heart and mind rooted in compassion, integrity, and awareness.

genuine meditation

Genuine meditation is not just a ritual which begins and ends at the cushion. We learn to be an engaged renunciate, an urban mystic, committed to embodying the qualities of compassion, understanding, and balance in all our thoughts, actions, and speech. In our formal meditation practice, we come to deeply understand that agitation, disconnection, and anxiety are optional. In the times of stillness on our cushion, we learn that the times of greatest turmoil and struggle in our minds and hearts are the times when we are most unconscious and unaware. This is equally true in our daily lives, and we come to see experientially that mindfulness and the willingness to learn illuminates all the moments when we become enmeshed in habit and reactivity.

1 Struggle begins to calm.

2 Habit is dissolved by sensitivity.

3 Unconsciousness disappears in the light of awareness.

Inner calm and understanding are just the beginning of our journey; we are invited to apply and embody peace, understanding, and compassion in

every moment of our life. Moments of profound illumination and insight on the meditative path are not confined to times of stillness on the cushion removed from the world.

engaging with the world

As you begin to integrate your meditation into daily life, you will find that some of the deepest awakenings in your meditative journey are when you are engaged with the world. The time we have spent developing our meditative practice on the cushion allows us to respond in ways that were previously not open to us.

Our formal meditation can help us in our daily lives to find clarity in confusion, peace in dissonance, calm amidst the chaos, and compassion in the face of suffering. Wise responsiveness, mindful attention, and receptiveness are the practical daily applications of insights we have discovered about the causes of anxiety, agitation, and turmoil in the course of our formal meditation.

from cushion to practice

The understandings we have explored in our formal meditation only become fully realized when they are applied to our daily encounters and activities. At these moments, we learn to approach our life with an openness and commitment to deepen in sensitivity, mindfulness, and wisdom.

cultivating our awareness

Cultivating our awareness is much more than just an abstract exercise. Meditation is not a passive journey. Mindfulness and insight can transform our lives, teaching us what it means to be a connected and conscious participant in each moment. We should never believe that all the small moments of calm, compassion, and mindfulness we nurture and embody in our lives do not matter. Each of our acts, thoughts, and choices can profoundly impact our world. It does not need more fear, hatred, and agitation. Our world is sorely in need of more compassion, wisdom, and peace.

life's joys and pleasures

Although meditation can bring profound happiness and contentment, its primary aim is to cultivate the understanding that liberates us from fear, hatred, and confusion. If the only aim of meditation were to create pleasurable states, it would be of limited value. Meditation allows you to appreciate more profoundly those pleasant and joyful moments that life brings. Equally, we will encounter moments in life that challenge us deeply. We may fall ill, come into conflict, or find ourselves feeling we are unable to cope, yet our meditative practice will allow us to meet these challenges with sensitivity, understanding, and wisdom. Our

meditative practice allows us to bring these qualities to the whole range of emotions and experiences that life brings; we are able to embrace elation and despair, praise and blame, and success and failure with balance.

We cannot ever hope to control everything that is taking place in our lives. Confusion, disorder, and unpredictability means that we need to learn to cultivate the willingness to approach unpleasant and difficult moments with the same understanding and attentiveness that we bring to moments of happiness and elation.

awareness and understanding

It would be unwise to see meditation as a ready-made or quick-fix solution to the challenges that we will inevitably encounter in our daily lives. Rather it is a path that teaches us the power of attentiveness and its capacity to transform the seemingly insurmountable into something that can be met with balance, calmness, and understanding. Moments such as this are effectively our "teachers," asking us to deepen our understanding and compassion.

Meditation will also help us to understand the difference between moments that require acceptance and understanding and those that demand wise and clear

responses. Meditation is not about creating a "perfect world" devoid of discomfort, fear, or pain. Rather it is a way of living in the real world with an awareness and understanding that transform all moments of our lives.

A BALANCED APPROACH

1 Mindfulness practice could be defined as a way of being and living in which all moments are greeted with equal respect and responded to with wholehearted attentiveness.

2 Living with a meditative spirit means deeply understanding the invitation of each moment in our life to embody all the care, peace, and intimacy we treasure. We learn not to reject anything as being insignificant or boring, understanding that meditation is learning to awaken our capacity to be connected with all things equally.

3 A meditative spirit dissolves the barriers we have erected between a "spiritual" and "worldly" life. A spiritual life can never be defined by how much time we spend in formal meditation, but by our willingness to learn, to bring healing where there is sorrow, and by our capacity to be touched deeply by all that life brings.

attentiveness in daily life

Cultivating attentiveness in the movements, events, and changes in our everyday lives requires the same dedication and perseverance as in formal meditation. At first, it may appear more difficult to maintain a clear attentiveness when surround by the bustle, noise, and unpredictability of the outside world. However, we are only asked to attend to one moment at a time. Just as in formal meditation, there will be countless moments when we find ourselves lost, distracted, or enmeshed in thought. Just as we have learned on the cushion, we can find the willingness to begin again. There may be many moments we find ourselves drawn into habitual speech, action, and reaction. We begin to know these moments more clearly. Rather than judging them or feeling disheartened, we come to trust that we can reclaim intimacy, wakefulness, and sensitivity.

For our practice to deepen and feel alive and vital, we need to approach our life in a holistic way, excluding nothing from the lens of our mindfulness. We all posses the capacity to be attentive and present, but only a few choose to develop this through practice and application. Formal meditation is the means to cultivate this attention, while in everyday life there are exercises to help us deepen our capacity for awareness and sensitivity. By accepting no separation between the everyday and the sacred, our life becomes our meditation room.

WILLINGNESS TO LEARN

A meditative life is ultimately about respecting and approaching each moment with a willingness to learn the lessons of connectedness, compassion, and peace. It can be easy to be peaceful when we find ourselves undisturbed, to be compassionate in the face of the suffering of those we love.

A MEDITATIVE LIFE WILL ASK US TO . . .

1 . . . be compassionate for those we do not love.

2 . . . find peace in the midst of disturbance.

3 . . . find understanding in the face of intolerance.

4 . . . commit ourselves to meeting each moment with an open heart and an inquiring spirit. Rather than dwelling on past events or future possibilities, we recognize that transformation can only take place in the present.

Many moments of our lives can be lost to habit, dwelling in the past, or living for the future. However, we can reclaim these moments by learning to be aware, mindful, and present.

mindful walking

Like breathing, walking is an integral part of our everyday lives. It is also something that we can perform habitually and unconsciously, intent only on arriving at our destination. Walking can also become an exercise in developing our attentiveness and mindfulness, where we learn to integrate our mind, body, and the present moment. The act of walking provides us with a focus with which to cultivate attentiveness while leading a busy life. We can use these times to reconnect with our bodies and simplicity.

As we walk between the rooms in our homes, to the bus stop, from one place to another, we are presented with a stream of opportunities to cultivate our attentiveness and mindfulness, and reclaim the moments that all too often become lost in the fog of habit.

Walking can now become an act of wakefulness and sensitivity, a moment of mindfulness. We come to realize at those moments when we find ourselves rushing and hurrying that our bodies are actually expressing our state of mind. This greater sensitivity and insight can help us to defuse the causes of stress and agitation. Undertaken with a meditative spirit, walking offers us a means to be present wherever we are, learning to rest in the moment and reconnect with our bodies. Instead of tilting toward the future, intent only on arriving, we learn that by calming the agitation of our bodies, we equally calm our hearts.

DEVELOPING ATTENTIVENESS WHILE WALKING

If you are in a tranquil space, listen attentively to your footfall, catching every broken twig or crushed leaf. Listen for the sound of birdcall, and focus on it.	Even in the heart of the city, pay attention to the sounds of traffic, and integrate them into your consciousness. In the heart of chaos while we walk, we can cultivate awareness.	Walk around your home, hearing the sounds of the space, taking in the scents of the different rooms, focusing on the objects you have chosen to introduce into your living space.	As you walk, focus on your body—your feet, legs, back, and torso. Feel every movement as you place one foot in front of the other. Listen to your breathing, making yourself aware of each in-breath and out-breath.

mindful walking continued

WALKING WITH AWARENESS

1 As you start your day, make a point of being aware of your body in all the movements you make while walking. Attend to the sensations that take place as you begin to move. As you stand, remind yourself to be aware that you are standing.

2 Sense the contact of your feet with the floor, the uprightness of your posture, and the feelings in your muscles as you stretch for the first time in the day. Now just take a moment to stand still, checking that your attention has not already leapt ahead to what you will be doing later in the day. If it has, bring your attention back to your body and let go of the preoccupation with what comes next.

3 As you begin to move, try to keep your attention focused on your body and anchored within the sensations you experience from moment to moment. Remain present with each step you take, aware of the different sights, sounds, and sensations that each step brings.

4 As you walk, move your attention down through your body, sensing the way your arms and legs move, and the weight of your body shifting with each step.

5 Try alternating your pace, first quickening and then slowing your pace slightly. Attend to the different sensations as you do this. You may begin to understand the way in which your walking is governed by habit. Give attention to those moments when you find your walking rushed or agitated, and notice the way in which these feelings isolate you from being present with your body.

6 Try letting go of this haste, slowing your pace and reconnecting with your body, being present in each step that you take. Once you arrive at your destination, take a moment to attend to the sensations in your body as you slow and then stop walking.

7 Listen to your breathing as it slows and returns to normal. Hold on to the sensations that walking has evoked.

mindful eating

Meditation is a process of deepening sensitivity in all the apparently "ordinary" activities of your life. Some of the most important parts of each day are when we prepare and eat food. Too often this elemental task is taken for granted and we become inured from understanding and being attentive to that moment. Often preparing and consuming food becomes a chore, a habit and distraction in our day; but it also can be a time of great sensitivity and awareness.

food and the mind

The food we eat and the way we eat it has a profound impact on our life not only in terms of physical nourishment but also in terms of our state of mind. We should take the time to be mindful of the fact that the food that arrives at our table is the result of the hard work of many people and the generosity of the natural world. For others, each meal is counted as a blessing and a means to survive. By being attentive while we eat, we acknowledge the abundance we enjoy while honoring those who struggle to survive each day.

eating habits

If we think about the ways we consume food, we will soon discover how much of our eating is performed habitually and unconsciously. Much of the time, we will find ourselves rushing, with food consumed merely to stave off our hunger. When we are preoccupied, we eat while pondering something else, disconnected from our bodies. Often when we are unhappy, we use food as a source of comfort, a diversion from whatever is causing sadness. Food often becomes a way of distracting ourselves from dealing with the source of sadness, anger, or confusion.

BENEFITS OF MINDFUL EATING

Mindful eating asks that we ensure that we sit down to eat, that it is a moment of calm during our day, and that we remain present as we taste, chew, and swallow, one bite at a time.

In much the same way as walking or breathing, the everyday act of eating is transformed when you bring a gentle awareness to it. Body, mind, and the present moment are unified in our attentiveness and this allows us to cultivate well-being and harmony.

The more attentive to each moment we become, the more natural and instinctive our awareness and understanding will be.

mindful eating continued

DEVELOPING MINDFUL EATING

As you sit down to eat, take a moment to sit quietly and relax your body. As you sit, bring a gentle awareness to the space surrounding you. Feel the contact of your body with the chair and the points of contact between the soles of your feet and the floor.

Now run your eyes over the food on the plate, taking the time to observe the different colors, shapes, smells, and textures of the food in front of you.

As you begin to eat, pay attention to the movement of your arms, hands, and torso as you pick up your cutlery and begin to cut and lift pieces of food. Sense the feeling of the flatware in your hand, sensing its weight, its feel, and its temperature.

As you begin eating, notice the sensation of taste as the food makes contact with your tastebuds. As you chew, be mindful of the taste and satisfaction the food is giving you.

When you find yourself anticipating the next bite, gently bring your attention back to sensations arising from the food you are eating at this moment. Try putting your cutlery down after each mouthful, and simply attend to the flavor and texture of the food in your mouth. As you swallow and begin to take the next mouthful be sure to stay present within the moment.

Eating is a time during our day that can be dedicated to appreciation and sensitivity. Attend to the change in your body from a state of hunger to a state of satisfaction. Stay present throughout this transformation, sensing it as it takes place, moment by moment, throughout the meal. Let your meal be a time dedicated to calmness and mindfulness.

At the point where you sense that your hunger has turned into satisfaction, acknowledge that you have eaten enough and stop. Attend to the feeling of satisfaction and completion in your body. Bring your attention into your body, sensing its ease.

Once again before you leave the table, take the time to attend to the feeling of your body against the chair, the points of contact between your feet and the ground, and the sights, sounds, and smells that surround you in that moment.

attaining simplicity

A reality of the world we live in is that we are constantly being fed messages that encourage us to consume more, do more, have more, and take more. We are told that happiness is an acquisitive life. Yet many of us are unfulfilled in the midst of consumption. Many different spiritual traditions have contended that happiness and fulfilment reside in our hearts and minds and not in what we can possess and gather.

Too often we feel burdened by the weight of all we have amassed and the need to defend and maintain it. For most of us, a life of greater simplicity and ease is directly linked to our willingness to let go of all that we do not truly need. Letting go does not mean not caring or a life of deprivation: it is a gift of compassion for ourselves.

A simpler life takes many forms. It does not demand that we forsake our possessions, home, jobs, or interests. Simplicity is about coming to embody and express understanding in all our actions. This is not about austerity but it is an ongoing series of questions throughout our lives that asks us to examine what makes us happy and what leads to anxiety and insecurity. Simplicity can be explored in nearly every aspect of our lives; our choices, actions, and speech offer opportunities to discover what gives us genuine happiness, ease, and spaciousness.

The cultivation of simplicity is one of the most direct ways of finding well-being, peace, and harmony. In cultivating simplicity in our lives and within ourselves, we can deepen our understanding of the world around us.

WE SHOULD ASK OURSELVES

1 Am I listening well?

2 Am I willing to be wholeheartedly present in my life?

3 Am I at ease in stillness and solitude?

4 Can I see, touch, and feel with a heart of openness and sensitivity?

5 Am I willing to meet this moment as it is rather than as I demand it should be?

6 Can I let go of my preoccupations with the past and future and attend to the moment I am living?

7 Where else will we find the depth, peace, and intimacy we treasure but here?

ELIMINATING EXCESS

Simplicity can also be cultivated by attending to the manner in which we live our lives. Recognizing that excessive stress, complexity, and confusion in our daily lives will inevitably be reflected in our consciousness, a meditative life asks us to make wise choices.

1 If we deeply value an open and sensitive heart, we may need to dedicate as much time to "being" as we dedicate to "doing."

2 Cultivate more moments of stillness in our days, more moments of calmness and listening in the culture of our lives.

3 Cultivating simplicity fundamentally alters our relationship with the world. Voluntary and conscious simplicity asks us to take from the world only what we truly need for our own well-being and the well-being of the world we live in.

4 Learning to let go of the greed and wanting that, rather than enriching us, simply entangles and restricts us.

Cultivating simplicity we find a deeper sense of compassion and interconnectedness. Sensitivity is rooted in simplicity; we need an open, uncluttered mind alive to the world around us.

attaining simplicity continued

1 As you begin your day, plant a seed of intention to attend to those moments when nothing seems to demand your attention. For example, as you walk to work or have a short break during the day.

2 At these times, attend to what is happening in your mind and body. When you find yourself seeking to fill that moment with a distraction—you may want to call someone, tidy something, ponder a past mistake, or plan the future—gently bring your attention back to your body and your breathing. Sense what it means to rest in those moments.

3 To start with, you may find the sensation of having "nothing to do" uncomfortable. You may feel you are "wasting time," and reach out to find something to do. Rather than responding to this impulse, bring your attention back to your body and mind.

4 Explore the unease that you are feeling, the sense that you must fill the space, and acknowledge it for what it is. Then reflect on the comfort that stillness brings and the space that nondoing can give you.

5 As we attend to this stillness and nondoing, we might find ourselves finally grasping how complex and busy our minds are from moment to moment. Rather than being drawn into this mass of conflicting thought, try instead just paying attention to how these streams of thoughts arise.

6 At those points in the day where you find yourself in a natural lull in activity, commit yourself to stillness and simplicity. Use this time to befriend your mind and body, letting go of tension and agitation, and explore the deep sense of ease that taking time to attend to the moment can evoke. Rather than focusing on what is missing, focus on what is there and what you do have.

7 As the capacity to feel at ease in stillness develops, you will find that it brings with it a greater sensitivity and awareness. Stillness and simplicity can be used as a resource for calm, creativity, and renewal. At these times, reflect on the objects that fill your life and ask yourself if they are necessary. Ask: *What am I holding onto out of fear and anxiety?* Do you really still need these things. Ask if letting go would make your life calmer, less anxious, simpler.

8 In these moments, also ask yourself if there is something that you frequently dwell on or obsess about. Try to explore if the spaciousness of your mind had been disrupted by unattainable goals, desires, and fantasies. Ask yourself if these things have really made a contribution to your sense of well-being. Reflect on the comfort that stillness can bring and the space that nondoing can give you.

9 Explore the way that you live your life and ask yourself where it could be simpler. Try to understand what you may be able to let go of in order to make your life less complex and anxiety ridden. Reflect on what a simpler life might look and feel like for you.

the practice of integrity

All meditative traditions place an emphasis on an ethical life. A heart of loving kindness provides the foundation for a mind and a life that are calm and happy. Genuine ethics are rooted in a sensitivity and awareness of how our actions impact on ourselves and others. Ethics applies to the actions, speech, and thoughts that reflect the state of our heart and mind moment to moment. The guiding principles of an ethical life are an understanding of what contributes to harm and suffering, and what relieves and heals it. An ethical life is rooted in an understanding of interconnectedness.

paying attention

Attention is our ally in seeking a practice of integrity, freeing us from impulses and habits rooted in fear and anger, allowing for the emergence of our innate compassion and kindness. In reflecting on what leads to conflict and disturbance and what leads to peace and understanding, we bring ourselves closer to a way of life characterized by sensitivity and integrity. Integrity is born of committing ourselves to bodily, verbal, and mental acts of loving kindness. The embodiment of this inner training is expressed in restraining from harmfulness, the commitment to truthfulness in our speech, integrity in our relationships, honesty in our actions, and the treasuring of a mind unclouded by intoxicants.

heartfelt communication

A vital part of this ethical approach is cultivating a sensitivity in our relationships that allows us to be open, receptive, and connected to the moment. The primary way in which we express ourselves and connect with others is through our speech, a vehicle of communication that holds immense power to foster either alienation or understanding. We can all recall a time when we have been deeply wounded by the words of another, and times when we have profoundly regretted words we have said. Our speech tends to be an area of our life in which we are most prone to be impulsive and unmindful. Our most intense emotions, thoughts, and states of mind are articulated through our speech, both those that are destructive and those that are most helpful and healing.

the wisdom of speech

Wise speech is in itself a meditative practice. Wise speech demands that we ask ourselves about what our intentions are when we speak.

- Are our words helpful or hurtful?
- Is our communication truthful?
- Is what we are telling this person useful to them?

These kinds of questions can help us to understand how we can communicate better and embody the qualities of openness, understanding, and wisdom

in what we say. We can learn to bring a mindful pause into the moment our words are about to be released, caring not only for our own well-being but for the well-being of the person we are relating to.

listening with openness

When you listen with openness to what another person is saying to you, you prove yourself to be:

- open to hearing something you may not have anticipated
- open to understanding the heart and mind of the person speaking to you

Notice when you begin to judge or dismiss the person speaking to you rather than listening to the entirety of what they have to say. It is particularly important that we are able to be receptive when someone is upset, hurt, or angry. Rather than being lost in their barrage of words or emotion, you could begin to sense all the ways in which they are communicating with you: their body language, tone of voice, facial expressions, and manner of speech, in addition to the words they are using. They may not always be asking you for solutions or answers but for your willingness to truly hear what they are communicating to you.

Be a compassionate presence—someone who listens with openness, honesty, and understanding.

MINDFUL LISTENING

Genuine communication is a two-way process, and a meditative life is one where we learn to be truly receptive and wholehearted in our listening. We often listen in only a perfunctory way, straining to find the moment when we can interject our own words.

1 To learn to listen deeply to another is to offer them our heartfelt respect and attention. The skill of listening to another develops simultaneously with the skill of listening to ourselves as we speak. Mindful listening requires immense patience, tolerance, and generosity.

2 Notice those moments when impatience or boredom leads you to disconnect from the person speaking to you. Gently bring your attention back to listening wholeheartedly with a clear intention to remain present.

3 Mindful listening is a path of cultivating the sensitivity, attentiveness, and warmth that are the foundations of every nurturing relationship.

mindful speech

PAYING ATTENTION TO YOUR OWN SPEECH

1 As you begin your day, set out with the clear intention to be mindful of those moments where you are communicating with others. Be aware of how normally your self-awareness changes from conversation to conversation. In some, you attend very closely to what is being said, while in others, you are distracted and simply going through the motions. Attempt to bring the same quality of attention to every conversation, big and small, that you have throughout your day.

2 Attend to the way in which you are speaking to those you may feel indifferent toward. This may be someone in a supermarket or asking you for directions. Rather than reverting to your habitual way of dealing with these people, try looking into their eyes as you speak. When you say something to them, do it with a sincerity and heartfelt desire to communicate. Determine whether it is possible, however briefly, to connect with that person.

3 Often, even when we are speaking with someone we love and care for, we find ourselves switching off and our mind wandering as we speak to them. We have become so used to their presence and we communicate so often that we have forgotten how special that person is and how important it is to convey this feeling in the way we speak and listen. Try to attend to the words you are using and the message they are conveying. Being sensitive to the way in which you speak to someone can convey a message of its own.

4 Similarly, be aware of your speech at those moments when you find yourself in the company of someone you dislike or who intimidates you. Give attention to your emotional landscape before speaking to ensure that what you are saying is honest, helpful, and not something you may regret. Ask yourself if it is possible to stay connected with the person whom you dislike or struggle with.

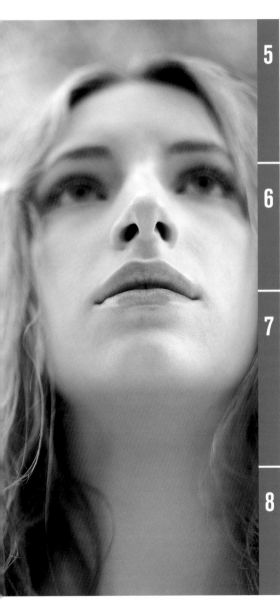

5 Bring awareness to your face, throat, lips, and eyes when you are speaking. Attend to what happens in those areas before and after you speak. Sense the physical changes in your body as the conversation takes place. Ask yourself what the messages you are receiving make you feel inside.

6 This awareness that we bring to our speech helps us to cultivate a way of communicating free from judgement and condemnation. Rather than impulsively reacting to what you are hearing, explore how what is being said makes you feel.

7 We should seek to cultivate restraint, so that we do not speak and then regret what we have said. This is important when entering situations that are charged with anger and anxiety. Yet it is also important to understand the difference between restraint and suppression: restraint asks us to be aware and to understand before we engage; suppression asks only that we do not express our feelings.

8 As you attend to your speech throughout the day, you will find that you communicate with greater clarity, simplicity, and compassion, and this can make speech a powerful tool for creating both intimacy and connectedness with others.

dissolving habit

Habits are easily gained but can be difficult to leave behind. A powerful way of deepening our awareness and sensitivity is to concentrate on and become aware of the ways in which we behave habitually. Try selecting one aspect of your life which you have taken for granted or are particularly unconscious of. This could be the way you relate to family and friends or something much simpler like how you eat, tie your shoes, or travel to and from work.

Commit yourself to approaching that activity as if it was the very first time you were doing it. Be aware of how you perform the action, the movements in your body, and the sensations that arise. If you are communicating with someone, pay attention to the way you speak and listen. It is not that there is a right or wrong way to perform these actions, rather an exploration of the activities and how they are transformed by attentiveness, sensitivity, and a commitment to being wholeheartedly present. As we become more attentive, we will find habit begins to dissolve and we are in connection with the moment. We are learning to see all things free from prejudices, assumptions, and opinions, and to understand their true nature in a compassionate, open way.

To live an awakened life is to challenge our habitual responses with interest and attention. Habit and wakefulness are rarely compatible. Habit leads to a life of assumptions and a lack of engagement with the moment we are actually in. Habit binds us to the past and distances us from the realities of our life. Mindfulness encourages us to approach our lives with a beginner's mind and innocent eyes, engaging with the present and unclouded by the past.

ENGAGING WITH THE MOMENT

Awareness is the cultivation of intimacy in each moment. Awareness teaches us that every single moment and every single activity in our day is worthy of our wholehearted attention.

Awareness has the capacity to break down our habitual responses and replace them with something that is spontaneous, open, and filled with understanding.

Awareness teaches us to move beyond our superficial assumptions and to take nothing in life for granted.

Awareness seeks to discover the possibilities of each moment and in doing so has the capacity to transform our lives, as we become aware of opportunities and outcomes we were previously all too ready to dismiss.

challenging habits

DEVELOPING A NEW CONSCIOUSNESS

1 Take a moment to reflect on your day-to-day life and think about all the ways in which you behave habitually. You might identify habit in some of the simple actions that you undertake—washing dishes, cleaning the car, or walking to work.

2 You may also see habit in any repetitive action that you have to perform on a day-to-day basis. Repetitive activities by their very nature encourage us to behave mechanically.

3 When you perform these activities, try to be aware of the huge range of physical sensations that accompany them. If you are washing the dishes, attend to the motions of your hands, the temperature of the water, and the different shapes and forms of the objects you are washing. If you are walking to work, think about the feeling of lifting your leg as you take each step, the contact that your foot makes with the ground and the sights, sounds, and smells of the environment that surrounds you.

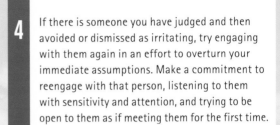

4 If there is someone you have judged and then avoided or dismissed as irritating, try engaging with them again in an effort to overturn your immediate assumptions. Make a commitment to reengage with that person, listening to them with sensitivity and attention, and trying to be open to them as if meeting them for the first time.

5 Sense what happens when you are willing to overturn immediate impressions and assumptions. Take time to form an opinion, so that it is considered rather than immediate, and a true reflection of your inner feelings.

6 At the beginning of each day, make a commitment to being fully present and aware in all activities during the day. Over time, this will allow a new depth and sensitivity to emerge.

reflection upon difficult circumstances

Meditation is not about avoiding or softening the blow of moments of conflict and difficulty that we are bound to encounter during our lives. Rather it is a means to approach these moments with clarity, understanding, and calm. We may be faced by a situation where conflict, hurt, and misunderstanding are burdens on our heart and mind. Conflict is transformed by forgiveness, tolerance, and generosity. The greatest conflicts demand the deepest understanding.

Different aspects of our attention can also be brought to bear on stressful situations. For example, before entering a situation that has caused repeated tension, try bringing your attention into your body and note how the situation is conditioning your response. Sense the way in which your body begins to tense up and your mind begins to fill with thoughts of aversion, fear, and resistance. Now use your attention to let your body relax as you reinterpret your feelings of anger and fear in light of an accepting attention. Once you find yourself immersed in the situation, keep bringing your attention back to the feelings in your body, consciously relaxing them. Sometimes we need to reflect on relationships that may be hurting others or ourselves.

Clearly, reflection is vital to making wise choices in difficult situations. What we must not confuse is repetitive and obsessive thinking with reflection: one allows us to move forward while

WE SHOULD ASK OURSELVES

1 *What is it that I need to let go of in order for this relationship to change?*

2 *Are there emotions rooted in the past that are preventing me from meeting this situation in the present with openness, understanding, and sensitivity?*

3 *Do I need to communicate more honestly and openly?*

4 *Am I able to approach the situation with compassion and understanding or do I need to develop these qualities further before seeking a resolution?*

the other denies us the ability to engage with the present. For the impossible to be transformed into the possible, we are asked to let go of resistance, prejudice, and assumptions.

reflective themes

Reflection is a powerful tool in the deepening of understanding and the integration of our path into our lives. Compassion, generosity, impermanence, or wise speech can all be themes to reflect on. As you rise in the morning, sow an intention in your mind to be aware of your speech as you go through the day, to sense beginnings and endings you experience, or to cultivate generosity and compassion. During the day, renew the intention so it is fresh in your mind. At the end of your day you can spend a few moments reflecting on how the theme you have chosen has arisen during your day and how you chose to relate to it.

We should not confuse a reflective theme with endless contemplation or self-consciousness of our actions. Rather, in selecting a them, we become increasingly aware of the way in which this theme informs and arises in our life.

The path of meditation is elegantly simple—seeking clarity, balance, peace, and freedom. It is not always easy: it asks for a dedication that can be renewed in moments of forgetfulness. We remember what it means to live with a wise and compassionate heart.

index

acknowledgments

The author would like to express her deep appreciation to Lucas Ochoa for his invaluable help in the preparation of this book.

Author photo: Libby Vigeon